Thomas Cromwell: Henry VIII's Chief Minister

A Tudor Times Insight

By Tudor Times

Published by Tudor Times Ltd

Tudor Times Insights

Tudor Times Insights are books collating articles from our website www.tudortimes.co.uk which is a repository for a wide variety of information about the Tudor and Stewart period 1485 – 1625. There you can find material on People, Places, Daily Life, Military & Warfare, Politics & Economics and Religion. The site has a Book Review section, with author interviews and a book club. It also features comprehensive family trees, and a 'What's On' event list with information about forthcoming activities relevant to the Tudors and Stewarts.

Titles in the Series

Profiles

Katherine Parr: Henry VIII's Sixth Queen

James IV: King of Scots

Lady Margaret Pole: Countess of Salisbury

Thomas Wolsey: Henry VIII's Cardinal

Marie of Guise: Regent of Scotland

Thomas Cromwell: Henry VIII's Chief Minister

Lady Penelope Devereux: Sir Philip Sidney's Muse

James V: Scotland's Renaissance King

Lady Katherine Grey: Tudor Prisoner

Sir William Cecil: Elizabeth I's Chief Minister

Lady Margaret Douglas: Countess of Lennox

Sir James Melville: Scottish Ambassador

Tudors & Stewarts 2015: A collection of 12 Profiles

People

Who's Who in Wolf Hall

Politics & Economy

Field of Cloth of Gold

Succession: The Tudor Problem

The Pilgrimage of Grace and Exeter Conspiracy

Contents

Introduction 6

Family Tree..7

Thomas Cromwell's Life Story..8

Aspects of Thomas Cromwell's Life 41

Bibliography 54

Thomas Cromwell: Henry VIII's Chief Minister

Introduction

Thomas Cromwell, son of a Putney blacksmith, rose to be the most powerful man in England after the King. A soldier, merchant, lawyer, politician and reformer, Cromwell cut a swathe through tradition to begin the transformation of England from a mediaeval country within Catholic Christendom, to a Protestant Nation State. His exceptional administrative ability made him indispensable to Henry VIII, and his political acumen helped him out-manoeuvre his many rivals. Like others before and after him, he eventually fell from power through entanglement with Henry's matrimonial problems.

In his youth, Cromwell travelled widely in Europe. After joining Wolsey's household, he spent much of his time in and around the south-east of England, attending to Wolsey's property matters. As Minister to Henry, he seldom went far from the King's side.

Cromwell has been a controversial figure for 500 years: ruthless schemer; visionary statesman; committed Protestant; destroyer of Queens and royal blood; saint and sinner. He was all of these and more; generous and supportive to friends, he made an implacable enemy.

Part 6 contains Thomas Cromwell's Life Story and additional articles about him, looking at different aspects of his life.

Family Tree

Thomas CROMWELL

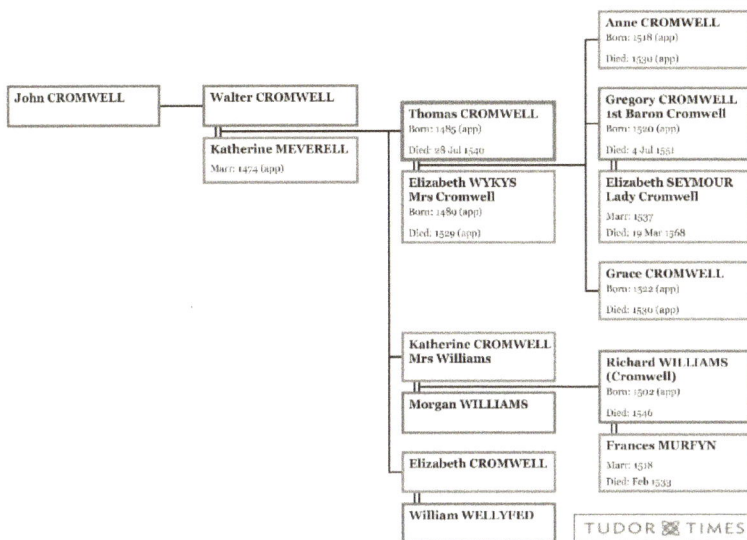

			Anne CROMWELL Born: 1518 (app) Died: 1530 (app)
John CROMWELL	**Walter CROMWELL**	**Thomas CROMWELL** Born: 1485 (app) Died: 28 Jul 1540	**Gregory CROMWELL 1st Baron Cromwell** Born: 1520 (app) Died: 4 Jul 1551
	Katherine MEVERELL Marr: 1474 (app)	**Elizabeth WYKYS Mrs Cromwell** Born: 1489 (app) Died: 1529 (app)	**Elizabeth SEYMOUR Lady Cromwell** Marr: 1537 Died: 19 Mar 1568
			Grace CROMWELL Born: 1522 (app) Died: 1530 (app)
		Katherine CROMWELL Mrs Williams	**Richard WILLIAMS (Cromwell)** Born: 1502 (app) Died: 1546
		Morgan WILLIAMS	**Frances MURFYN** Marr: 1518 Died: Feb 1533
		Elizabeth CROMWELL	
		William WELLYFED	

TUDOR TIMES

© Tudor Times Ltd 2014

Thomas Cromwell's Life Story

Chapter 1: Early Life (c. 1485 – 1512)

Thomas Cromwell was born around 1485 to Walter Cromwell and his wife, Katherine Meverell. Walter was a blacksmith, brewer and tradesman in the district of Putney, south London, although the Cromwells originally came from Norwell in Nottinghamshire. The family was reasonably prosperous, and Walter served in the usual local offices of juryman and constable. However, he often fell foul of the law himself, and was repeatedly fined for breaking the assize of ale, brawling and even fraud. Tradition has it that Cromwell and his father were on poor terms, but whether that is true or not, he was certainly on good terms with his sisters, as evidenced by his later support of their families.

The level of education Cromwell received formally is unknown – given his class and background it is likely he would have been sent to school to read, write and pick up some Latin, as well, of course, as being taught the practice of his religion. At some time, perhaps around the turn of the century, he left England for Europe. The Imperial Ambassador, Chapuys, claimed this was following a brief spell of imprisonment, and Cromwell himself told Archbishop Cranmer that he had been a 'ruffyan...in his younger days'. Other sources say it was owing to falling out with his father. Maybe both, or neither, are true.

Over the following years Cromwell became, first, a mercenary in the French army, involved in the terrible defeat the French suffered at Garigliano in December 1503, and second, the servant of an Italian merchant. A near-contemporary account says that the merchant found

Cromwell begging in the street, and, recognising an Englishman far from home, took pity on him and helped him. The merchant in question was Frescobaldo Frescobaldi, head of the eponymous Florentine banking house. The Frescobaldis had been bankers to English and other European kings since the twelfth century, and had an office and wide network in London. Cromwell's master, in fact, spent most of his time in London, although Cromwell entered his service in Florence. Whilst in the service of the banker, Cromwell not only picked up his phenomenal business acumen, but also developed tastes and interests that influenced him for the rest of his life. Exposed to the art and literature of Renaissance Italy, and particularly of Michelangelo, who traded works for wine with Frescobaldi, he acquired an interest in the new artistic styles in painting and production of high-quality, beautiful items. He continued to be a lover of Italian culture for the rest of his life. The same chronicler (Bardello) who told the story of his meeting with Frescobaldi describes Cromwell as

'quick-witted and prompt of resolution, knowing excellent well to accommodate himself to the wishes of others, and could...dissemble his purpose better than any man in the world.'

Nothing in his later life gives the lie to this description!

Cromwell is next heard of working with a cloth-merchant in Antwerp, perhaps in connection with Frescobaldi's business, or perhaps for the chance to learn about a trade that was extremely important to England and thus might give opportunities for the future. Once he had learnt enough, he began to trade on his own account.

Chapter 2: Developing a Career (1512 – 1522)

On his return to England, probably around the end of 1512, Cromwell began to practise law, his speciality being conveyancing. Again, where, or even if, he received formal training is unknown. However, he still maintained his connection with the cloth trade, making several trips to Antwerp and the other Burgundian cities. He also travelled to Rome in 1514, staying in the English hostel and appearing before the Papal Court on 29th May, giving evidence in a dispute between two English clergy. It has been speculated that Cromwell was undertaking this in the course of employment by Cardinal Bainbridge, Archbishop of York, but he is not formally recorded as in the Archbishop's household.

Not long after settling back in England, Cromwell married Elizabeth Wykys, a widow with a comfortable inheritance, and connections to the court, her father having been a Gentleman Usher to Henry VII. Whilst marriage for love alone was completely foreign to the sixteenth century mind, it was expected that married couples should love and care for each other. As she was widowed, Elizabeth Wykys might have been guided in the choice of a second husband by her father, but would have had a high degree of freedom in selection. Cromwell, too, was a free agent. We can therefore infer that they were happy to marry. The Cromwells had a son, and two, or possibly three, daughters. All of the daughters died young, but the son, Gregory, survived, and had an interesting career of his own.

In the 1500s and 1510s a strong wave of *'anticlericalism'* was spreading through London – a feeling of antagonism towards some of the more corrupt and questionable practices of the priests and other officials of the Catholic Church. It was not, initially, a question of disputes around doctrine, more of the way in which the clergy conducted themselves. This resentment was particularly prevalent amongst the mercantile and trading classes – the butchers, brewers, blacksmiths and tailors, amongst whom Cromwell had spent his youth, and with which he had ties, and the more prosperous cloth-merchants, importers and exporters who were his clients. It seems likely, from his later actions, that Cromwell, too, subscribed to the view that corruption and venality were widespread. Nevertheless, his private religious views, whatever they might have been at this stage, did not prevent him from taking a commission in 1517 from the Guild of the Church of Our Lady in St Botolph, Boston (now known as the Boston Stump).

Cromwell obviously had an aptitude for languages. Following his years in Europe, he spoke French and Italian fluently as well as Spanish (although how he picked that up is a mystery) and some German. Presumably he also had Flemish in his repertoire. His Latin and Greek, too, were commendable – Greek being a very rare accomplishment, and usually confined to academic circles. This fluency in other languages may have been a factor in obtaining commissions outside England.

The Guild sent Cromwell to Rome as a support and guide for their representative, Geoffrey Chambers, on a mission to the Pope. The mission was successful and the story of how Cromwell achieved his aims gives an insight into his methods that illustrates his way of working throughout his life. He spent some time discovering the Pope, Leo X's, tastes and interests. Accordingly, whilst most petitioners had to wait months to be heard, Cromwell arranged to waylay the Pope early one morning, with a trio of singers and a plate of marmalade and other delicacies prepared in the English fashion. The pope whose '*holy tooth greatly delighted in new-fangled strange delicacies and dainty dishes*' munched through the sweets, and granted the Guild's petition to renew the Indulgences that brought in income to maintain their church. Cromwell had learnt a valuable lesson – finding the right route to pleasing the powerful gets results.

It is not clear how Cromwell came to the notice of Cardinal Wolsey, perhaps through work done for Cardinal Bainbridge, Wolsey's predecessor as Archbishop of York, or it may have been from legal business he was involved in, although there is no firm, dateable evidence showing when Cromwell began practising law. His biographers differ widely in dating the beginning of the connection, from as early as 1516, by Elton, to as late as 1524 which Everett demonstrates is the earliest provable date. Looking at all the different arguments, a date of around 1519 would seem not unlikely. Working for Wolsey, did not, however, preclude him from other employment, and he is referred to in 1522 as a servant of Thomas Grey, Marquess of Dorset, a former pupil of Wolsey's and later, as Dorset's attorney.

Chapter 3: Councillor to My Lord Legate (1523 – 1530)

In 1523 Cromwell was returned as a Member of Parliament, probably owing to Wolsey's influence. Although the constituency for which he sat is not recorded, it is thought to be Bath. This was Cromwell's first appearance on the public stage, and the draft of the speech he prepared makes interesting reading, although we cannot know whether it was actually delivered. The purpose of the Parliament was to raise a subsidy for yet another French campaign and Cromwell's speech argues vigorously against it, citing the difficulties of war in a foreign land; the cost; the danger of a king with no son, and only an eight-year-old daughter as heir, adventuring himself in warfare; and most of all, the pointlessness of the exercise. He refers to Henry VIII's previous conquests as having *'cost His Highness more than twenty such ungracious dogholes could be worth to him'*

Everett argues that Cromwell preparing a speech so antithetical to government policy demonstrates that he could not have been working for

Wolsey. The counter-argument is that, as Wolsey was himself against further hostilities with France, he used Cromwell to point out the shortcomings of the policy.

Cromwell's later achievements relied heavily on Parliamentary process, however he was aware of its flaws, writing in amused tones to a friend that:

> 'we communed of war, peace, strife, contentation, debate, murmur, grudge, riches, poverty, perjury, truth, falsehood, justice, equity, deceit, oppression, magnanimity, activity, force, attemperance, treason, murder, felony, conciliation and also how a commonwealth might be edified. However, in conclusion we have done as our predecessors have been wont to do, that is to say, as well as we might and left where we began.'

In 1524, Cromwell was sufficiently respected in the legal profession to be nominated as a member of Gray's Inn, one of the Inns of Court, despite his lack of formal training. No doubt his position as 'Councillor to my Lord Legate (Wolsey)' helped his acceptance into a profession as conservative then as it is now.

By 1525, Wolsey was relying on Cromwell to a considerable extent. Not the least of his responsibilities was the suppression of some thirty monasteries (with Papal consent), the incomes of which were to found Wolsey's colleges at Ipswich and Oxford.

In undertaking his master's orders, Cromwell made himself hugely unpopular. He approached the task with a zeal for destruction of shrines that foreshadowed the events of the 1530s. The actual scope of his task was to survey the property, value it, prepare detailed inventories of the moveable goods and arrange for them to be taken away and sold. The inmates had to be either given pensions, or have arrangements made for them to be transferred to other religious houses. Cromwell, together with his two assistants, Sir William Gascoigne and Dr Allen, carried out the work efficiently and with dispatch – indeed a sense of urgency and decisiveness characterises all his activity.

The thirty foundations dissolved, it was time to move on to the construction of the two colleges, and Cromwell was again in charge. By April 1528, he could write to Wolsey that

'the buildings of your noble college most prosperously doth arise...the like thereof was never seen nor imagined, having consideration to the largeness, beauty, sumptuous, curious and most substantial building of the same.'

It was customary in the Tudor age for people to conduct business in a way we could consider corrupt. Gifts and sweeteners that we might call bribes, were commonplace. Thus, it was expected that Cromwell would line his own pocket whilst working for Wolsey, through such matters as granting a tenancy to the bidder who gave him the highest fee, or not accounting for all of the sales. Nevertheless the scale of embezzlement seems to have provoked an outcry and *'incredible things'* were reported to the King.

Despite the amount of work Cromwell was doing for Wolsey, he continued to practise law, and gave advice in a case for Lady Clere, the aunt of Anne Boleyn, regarding an action for debt, as well as being involved in numerous other petitions, arbitrations and daily legal matters.

During the 1520s, Cromwell developed an ever-widening circle of friends. He hosted dinners at his home in Austin Friars, in London, and later at Stepney, and his hospitality and generosity to his friends was widely praised. His guests, the lawyers and merchants of London, not only talked business, but also of church reform. In particular, they talked of the desire to have the Gospel in English.

Cromwell lost his wife, Elizabeth Wykys, in 1527 or 1528, probably to the sweating sickness. Unusually, Cromwell did not remarry, and there is no record of any long-term relationship with another woman. His daughters, Anne and Elizabeth, also died at some point between 1529, when he made a Will, and 1532 when he updated it. His son, Gregory, however, flourished, although there are hints in Cromwell's correspondence that Gregory, although a diligent scholar, did not have his father's quickness of intellect.

Throughout Cromwell's service with Wolsey, he was concerned only with the Cardinal's private business and legal affairs, and was not employed on any state business although he can hardly have been unaware of the *'King's Secret Matter'* – the quest for annulment of the marriage of Henry VIII and Katharine of Aragon. The first task Cromwell performed in any way connected with the case was not until 1529, and even then it was a matter of looking for the paperwork relating to Wolsey's position as Legate, to show to the King's attorney.

As the King's favour towards Wolsey waned, his enemies (of whom the chief were the Dukes of Norfolk and Suffolk) began to circle. Nevertheless, although the writing was on the wall for Wolsey, Cromwell continued to serve him faithfully, giving the best advice he could and staying with him longer than many of his other servants. Wolsey's Gentleman Usher and biographer, George Cavendish, records a scene at the Cardinal's home at Esher, whence he had been sent into a sort of exile. Cavendish greeted Cromwell who was

'...leaning in the great window...saying Our Lady Matins (which had since been a very strange sight). He prayed not more earnestly than the tears distilled from his eyes...."Why Master Cromwell, what meaneth all this your sorrow? Is my lord in any danger for whom you lament thus? Or is it for any loss that ye have sustained...?"

"Nay", quoth he. "...I am like to lose all that I have travailed for all the days of my life, for doing of my master true and diligent service....and this I understand right well, that I am in disdain with most men for my master's sake and surely without first cause...I intend, God willing, this afternoon when my Lord has dined to ride to London an so to the Court where I will either make or marr."'

Accordingly, Cromwell, with his personal clerk, Ralph Sadler, set off for London. A Parliament had been called, but up until this point, it does not appear that Cromwell had looked for a seat. Via a chain of connections, the Duke of Norfolk, the Lord Treasurer, was persuaded to ask the King if he would be happy for Cromwell to be in the House. (Although the King did not nominate members, it was certainly the practice of the chief nobles of the realm to present their own candidates for election by their tenants, so Parliament was not a widely democratic body).

On this occasion, Henry was happy that Cromwell should take a seat as a *'burgess"*. There was a general scurrying around to find a suitable place, and Cromwell was returned for Taunton, a seat within the influence of the Bishopric of Winchester, which had been one of Wolsey's clerical offices.

Chapter 4: The End of Cardinal Wolsey (1529 – 1530)

The Parliament called in 1529, that sat until 1536, is known as the *'Reformation Parliament'* and it would prove to be one of the most important ever assembled in England. During it, Henry VIII, ably assisted, if not led by Cromwell, changed the face of the nation for ever.

One of the first debates was in regard to a *'Book of Articles'* brought forward by Thomas Howard, 2nd Duke of Norfolk and Wolsey's inveterate enemy. Norfolk sought to have Wolsey condemned by an Act of

Attainder, obviating the need for trial. Cromwell argued passionately, and successfully, against the Book. The charges were dropped, and in February of 1530, Wolsey was granted a general pardon by the King. During this whole period, Wolsey wrote long, trusting letters to Cromwell and George Cavendish recorded that

> 'There could nothing be spoken of against my Lord in the Parliament House, but he (Cromwell) would answer it incontinent ...at length, for his (Cromwell's) honest behaviour in his Master's cause, he grew into such an estimation in every man's opinion, that he was esteemed to be the most faithful servant of his master...wherein he was of all men greatly commended.'

Despite this positive assessment by Cavendish, Cromwell's biographers differ in their treatment of his actions during 1529 and 1530 in regard to his support of Wolsey. Borman and Williams take his continued support of Wolsey at face value, but Robert Hutchinson gives a very much more cynical view, citing numerous letters where Wolsey begs for Cromwell to visit him, and points out that many of Cromwell's actions can be seen as advancing his own cause – for example, Wolsey, realising that Anne Boleyn's influence was growing ever stronger, wanted advice on what to do about it. Cromwell suggested that presents for her and her family would not come amiss, and, accordingly, Wolsey granted several pensions to the Boleyn family out of his estates as Bishop of Winchester. Hutchinson suggests that Cromwell was eager to take the credit with the Boleyns for these favours.

Elton's view is that, as soon as was compatible with decency, Cromwell sought out the King's service. Everett makes the interesting point that we are looking at the matter with hindsight – in the period 1529 - 1530 people could not know that Wolsey was doomed – Henry's behaviour was certainly ambivalent, and, given the King's genuine affection for Wolsey, and their long history together, it was certainly not impossible that the Cardinal could stage a come-back. Although Henry had shown himself ruthless in dispatching one or two of his nobles, the wholesale executions of wives and former favourites was yet to come. Cromwell may therefore have simply been continuing business as usual, until the time came when he had to choose between staying with the Cardinal when he was sent to live in his archdiocese of York, and remaining in London, perhaps to plead for Wolsey, or, by that time, to try to advance his own career.

The next stage of Cromwell's career is rooted in the work he did for Wolsey. As the man who arranged the founding and building of Wolsey's Colleges, and managed the Cardinal's financial and property business, he was the individual with the most knowledge and understanding of the complex legal issues surrounding the lands of the Colleges, and also Wolsey's other property, most notably York Place.

Strictly speaking, York Place belonged to the Archdiocese of York, not to the Cardinal. Henry, however, had taken a distinct fancy to it, and decided to appropriate it to build a new palace. He also wanted to use some of the revenues and lands belonging to York Place and other church lands to make grants to courtiers he wished to reward. The Tudor age was extremely legalistic and litigious. It was important that land grants were correctly made (and this involved a great deal of copying, stamping, signing, witnessing, sealing and use of correct terminology) or disputes would arise. As it was ecclesiastic land, there was some uncertainty as to the long term validity of any grants made by the King out of York Place's revenues. At the very least, it was thought that Wolsey needed to endorse some of the grants.

Cromwell was able to use of his legal skills and intimate knowledge of the Cardinal's lands to smooth the way for recipients. These activities brought him into regular contact with the King, as for example, when

Henry wanted to grant Lord Scales an office in Wolsey's gift. Cromwell was requested to draft a letter for the King to send to Wolsey. In these legal matters, there was much profit to be made as suitors promised fees and pensions to Cromwell to have their matter treated expeditiously. The King was impressed, and, as Sir John Russell wrote to Cromwell, '*the King's Grace had very good commendation of you.*'

At some point between February and April of 1530 this good impression was translated into a concrete reward, as Cromwell was officially retained as a servant of the King. Nevertheless he was still acting for Wolsey, and gave the Cardinal excellent advice, as, comforted by merely being banished to York, Wolsey could not help himself becoming embroiled in levels of display and extravagance that were bound to cause questions to be asked. The deal, whether or not explicitly stated to Wolsey, was that he would be allowed to retire quietly, provided no-one ever heard of him again. Cromwell told Wolsey to restrain his passion for building and content himself with a quiet life, advice Wolsey spectacularly failed to follow. In the last letter between them, Cromwell takes Wolsey firmly to task for having said or written something injurious to Cromwell – perhaps Wolsey believed he had been betrayed by his old servant. Cromwell was offended

'Truly your Grace in some things over shooteth yourself. There is a regard to be given what things you utter and to whom...'

Hutchinson believes that Cromwell had, in fact, betrayed the Cardinal and that his indignation was feigned.

Whatever the truth of the matter, Wolsey's death on 29th November 1530 released Cromwell from any lingering bonds of service and within a few weeks he was appointed to the King's Privy Council. According to Cavendish, on his promotion to the Council, Sir Thomas More, Lord Chancellor, advised him

'...in your counsel giving unto His Grace, ever tell him what he ought to do, but never what he is able to do. So shall you shew yourself a true faithful servant and a right worthy councillor. For if a lion knew his own strength, hard were it for any man to rule him.'

Chapter 5: In the King's Service

As well as spending more time with the King and his ministers, during 1531 Cromwell continued to immerse himself in legal activities, acting for the King in property matters, but not yet fully involved in policy making. He was not, in 1530, involved in the annulment, and without the Cardinal, it appeared that Henry did not know quite how to progress the case. One action the King set in motion was to send Thomas Cranmer, a Fellow of Cambridge, to collect the opinions of the theologians at the various European universities.

He also made a personal appeal to Charles V, but, with a lack of tact that is quite extraordinary, sent George Boleyn, Viscount Rochford, Anne's brother to make the plea. If Charles V were going to be persuaded to turn a blind eye to his aunt's humiliation, sending the brother of the *'other woman'* was not likely to be the most successful method.

By mid-1530, however, the King had a new idea – perhaps he did not need the Pope's ruling at all. After all, had not English Kings always been supreme in their own realm? Fifteen of the senior clergy were indicted for the crime of *'praemunire'* (obeying a foreign power, rather than the King). To avoid conviction, the Convocation of Clergy (the Church's governing body, subject in spiritual matters only to the Pope) on 24th January 1531 offered Henry the enormous sum of £100,000 in token of its penance.

They acknowledged that he was the Supreme Head of the Church in England, although the caveat *'as far as the law of God allows'* was hastily tacked on. Cromwell has been credited with putting the notion into Henry's head, but there is no evidence at all supporting that – no letters and no memoranda, which is not, of course, proof in itself, but given the amount of correspondence and paperwork that exist relating to Cromwell it is likely some note would be there.

Nevertheless, Cromwell's influence was growing and by the middle of 1531 he appears to have been involved in drafting bills to be placed before the Parliamentary session that opened in January 1532. The bills ranged from procedural matters about the import of bow-staves to further measures to curb the power of the Church. Following the payment of the aforementioned fine by Convocation, an act was introduced *'forgiving'* both clergy and laity. Cromwell seems to have worked with another of Henry's advisers, the lawyer, Thomas Audley, Speaker of the House in the Reformation Parliament, on drafting bills.

An early scheme for solving the annulment issue was suggested – the supremacy of the Archbishop of Canterbury over the English bishops would be invested in Convocation instead, thus enabling Convocation to grant the annulment that Archbishop Warham would not. Henry himself felt this was too controversial, and, instead, decided that a threat to the Pope's purse would be more effective.

A bill to stop the payment of *'first fruits and annates'* (the first year's income for a new bishop, customarily paid to the Pope) was introduced, although Cromwell seems to have been somewhat dubious about its efficacy. A clause was added, to keep the Act in abeyance until the King implemented it by letters patent, which demonstrates that even as late as Spring 1532, Henry still hoped that the Pope would grant his annulment. Despite the anti-clerical stance of the Commons, only Henry's personal intervention, through a visit to the Lords, got the bill through the Upper House.

The House of Lords may have had misgivings about attacks on Rome and the Church, but the Commons had the bit between their teeth. In 1529, Cromwell had drafted a series of complaints against the Clergy on behalf of the Commons that was now developed further into the 'Supplycacion against the Ordinaries (Ecclesiastic supervisors)' of 1532.

This 'Supplycacion' was a petition from the Commons to the King to control the powers of the Church. There is debate over whether the petition was spontaneous and truly represented the feeling of the Commons, or whether it was set up by the King, using Cromwell as his tool. As noted before, London, in particular, had a strong anti-clerical feeling so it may be that the King, whose intelligence and political acumen is often underrated, saw an opportunity to put further pressure on the Pope by listening to the Supplycacion.

After a lengthy preamble in which the Commons alleged that dissension was being sown, not only by the growth of 'heretical opinions', but, more substantially by the 'uncharitable behaviour of the Ordinaries' the Supplycacion puts forward various complaints that Parliament wished the King remedy. These included, conveniently for the King, a complaint against the authority of Convocation. Convocation was too powerful, and used its authority in arbitrary fashion.

In support of the view that the Supplycacion did really emerge from the Commons, Henry did not immediately act, but requested a reply from Convocation. In April 1532, when Convocation reconvened it had prepared an answer against the Supplycacion. The meat of Convocation's reply was that scripture upheld its position as a law-making body. Individual failings of clergy did not negate the laws of the Church. Regardless of whether he had been behind the Supplycacion or had just decided to use this new tool that had fallen into his hands, Henry was not satisfied.

On 10th May 1532, Convocation was required to assent to three articles that effectively established royal authority over them. In essence, Convocation could only make and enforce canon law with royal assent. The following day, the King made a speech in Parliament saying that he now saw that the clergy were but '*half his subjects*' and that their allegiance to Rome was contrary to their allegiance to him, but that he was sure the Commons, being '*a great sort of wise men*' would know how to act. Cromwell and Audley drew up a plan for Convocation, acceptance of which would require it to submit all of the existing Canon law to the King for approval, after it had been vetted by a committee of Clergy and Commons, and any items repugnant to the law of England deleted.

Warham's compromise suggestion was refused and on 16th May 1532, the Convocation of Clergy submitted itself to Crown jurisdiction. As the Imperial Ambassador, Chapuys noted, Convocation was now less than the guild of cobblers, as the cobblers could at least manage their own guild and make rules for it. On 17th May, Sir Thomas More resigned the Chancellorship, and was replaced by Audley.

Chapter 6: Increasing Influence (1532 – 1534)

Although from January 1532 Cromwell seems to have had the role of managing the King's business in the Commons, he was still busy with other work, including overseeing building works at the Palace of Westminster and the Tower of London, for both of which he had comprehensive responsibilities in managing construction, and auditing the accounts.

He also acted as Receiver General for what had previously been Cardinal College, Oxford, but was now to be re-founded as King Henry VIII's College. During this period, Cromwell was closely involved in financial and administrative matters relating to the King's revenues from vacant bishoprics or other ecclesiastical payments due to the Crown.

It was in April 1532 that Cromwell received his first official position, as Master of the King's Jewels, and shortly afterwards the low-key, but useful, Clerkship of the Hanaper – this brought in a fee every time a patent was sealed. His third office, nowhere near as important as it is today, was as Chancellor of the Exchequer. This trio of offices, although none was particularly significant in itself, gave him a spread of influence across the King's Household, the legal department of Chancery and the Exchequer. One of his early tasks as Master of the King's Jewels was to call in the plate that had Katharine of Aragon's arms as queen on it, for melting down.

Cromwell's next three appointments, as Principal Secretary in 1534, Master of the Rolls in 1534 and Lord Privy Seal in 1536, gave him oversight of the departments that executed government business. Although the Principal Secretaryship was not officially his until 1534, he began acting in that capacity in 1532, when the Secretary, Gardiner, was abroad on various diplomatic missions. Gardiner and Cromwell, from an early career together in Wolsey's household were, by now, at daggers drawn. Whether this was personal dislike, resentment by Cromwell at how easily Gardiner had abandoned Wolsey for the King, increasing distance on religious matters or mutual envy of the other's proximity to the King, can only be guessed at, but their rivalry continued until the downfall of one of them....

Prior to Cromwell's appointment, the role of Principal Secretary had not been especially important or prestigious – previous great ministers such as Wolsey, or Cardinal Morton in Henry VII's reign, had based their influence on the Lord Chancellorship, but from Cromwell's time to the current day, the position of Secretary of State has been one of the great offices in English, then UK government.

It is this period as Secretary that has furnished the enormous mass of correspondence on which much of our knowledge of the 1530s is based – it should, however be noted, as Cromwell's biographer Everett points out, that this might lead us to exaggerate Cromwell's level of influence. If we had records of other members of the court, a different picture might emerge.

This comprehensive management of administration, never concentrated in one man before, is the basis of the interpretation by the great Tudor historian, Geoffrey Elton, of Cromwell as leading a 'Revolution in government'. Elton portrays Cromwell as deliberately undertaking the transformation of the rather ramshackle machinery of mediaeval government into a sleek, well-ordered, bureaucracy.

Over the following years, Cromwell remained close to the King at all times. Unlike Wolsey, or his rivals, Norfolk and Gardiner, he seldom left London, other than to travel with the King on his summer progresses. It is apparent that, although he had clerks whom he trusted completely, in particular, his nephew Richard Williams (later called Cromwell) and Ralph Sadler, he was no delegator. His friend in Antwerp, Stephen Vaughan, wrote warning him that constant 'travail of common causes' would impair his judgement for greater things, and that 'by overmuch paining his body and cumbering his wits' he would sink into an early grave.

The voluminous documentation that charts Cromwell's activity is almost entirely business – there is very little to give a picture of Cromwell as a personality – although his friendship for Sir Thomas Wyatt peeps out of a letter. Records also show that he enjoyed hunting and hawking and kept greyhounds. He could draw a fine bow, and played bowls, cards and dice, gambling for high stakes as was common with all Henry's court.

He wined and dined his friends, ordering supplies of wine from Lord Lisle, in Calais, and employed musicians to entertain them.

The breadth of Cromwell's reading matter is, of course, unknown, but certain works of politics he definitely read, including Aristotle's '*Politics*' and Marsiligio of Padua's '*Defensor Pacis*'. We can infer, too, that he read Tyndale's '*On the Obedience of a Christian Man*' that so beguiled Henry and Anne Boleyn. Many biographers have referred to Cromwell as '*Machiavellian*', and claimed that he was a devotee of Machiavelli's work, and perhaps even knew him in Florence in his time there. Whilst any resident of Florence would have had to go round with his hands over his ears NOT to be aware of Machiavelli in the early 1510s, their different social status would preclude any meeting. There is no certainty that Cromwell read '*The Prince*' before receiving it as a gift in 1536.

By the end of 1532, the annulment was reaching crisis point. Anne Boleyn had finally surrendered her body to the King, and he was determined to marry her. More's resignation of the Chancellorship, and the death of Warham, Archbishop of Canterbury, in August 1532 finally paved the way out of the impasse. This was to be Cromwell's moment for obtaining Henry's heart's desire through legal means.

The first step was to obtain Cranmer's confirmation as Archbishop of Canterbury. Cranmer, an apparently innocuous Fellow of Cambridge, was nominated by Henry in October 1532, and approved by Clement VII in an effort to show Henry that the Papacy was trying to be accommodating. The new Archbishop was consecrated on 30th March 1533. Cromwell had helped to draft a protestation that Cranmer then immediately made, stating that his oath to the Pope could not bind him against God's Law, or the King's prerogative.

The second step was to pass the Act in Restraint of Appeals. This Act, again drafted by Cromwell, began with a long and convoluted preamble emphasising that England was an '*empire*' and thus not subject to any external authority, not even that of the *'Bishop of Rome'*. In consequence, ecclesiastical matters such as matrimony and legitimacy were to be tried and answered within the kingdom, with no appeal. Cromwell, as a master of Parliamentary business, was careful to work with lawyers and clergy through the drafting stage, taking alterations and amendments to give the Act the best possible chance of being passed. In the event, there was very little opposition, although Archbishop Lee of York, and Gardiner, Bishop of Winchester remained opposed.

As well as preparing the Act carefully, Cromwell managed the by-elections that had occurred since Parliament was summoned in 1529, to return members favourable to the King. He also urged all supporters to attend the vote, and discouraged any suspected of not being one hundred per cent on-side, such as Sir George Throckmorton of Coughton, a stout supporter of Katharine of Aragon, from coming to Parliament on the day of the vote. There was some debate in the Commons – merchants feared that the rest of Christendom might not wish to trade with a country that had left the umbrella of Papal Supremacy. Nevertheless, the Act was carried with a majority.

Convocation, headed by Cranmer, and now the supreme ecclesiastical body in England, declared Henry and Katharine's marriage to have been void *ab initio*, and his marriage to Anne legal. Cromwell had succeeded where Wolsey had failed.

Chapter 7: Dealing with Dissent (1534 – 1535)

The final annulment of Henry's first marriage brought the case of Elizabeth Barton, known as the *'Nun of Kent'*, to a head, and Cromwell was involved in the examination and punishment of an alleged group of traitors. Barton, a serving-woman in Canterbury, began to have visions of the Virgin Mary and other saints in 1525, following a serious illness. She was examined by the local priest and Archbishop Warham himself. Found to be a woman of virtue and blameless life, she was encouraged to become a nun. Over the following years, her prophecies and visions drew a large audience. She was even consulted by Wolsey and the King himself.

Barton's prophecies were all very conservative, discouraging Lutheranism, and supporting traditional practices – pleasing to Henry in a time when he was strongly anti-Lutheran himself. However, as the annulment case became public knowledge, Barton preached against it and drew the wrath of Henry down on both herself, and any who had listened to her. The list of her patrons included a number of high-ranking courtiers who were supporters of Katharine of Aragon, including Bishop Fisher of Rochester and Gertrude, Marchioness of Exeter.

The Nun was arrested and accused not only of leading an immoral life, but also of having made up her prophecies, under the orders of her priests. In a shameless display of greed, one of the chief accusers was Friar John Laurence who gave evidence against both her, and several of his brother friars, whilst asking to be granted the office that one of the accused would no longer need after being hanged. The Nun and five others were hanged at Tyburn and her supporters in court circles were under suspicion for some time.

Henry's chief objective of marriage to Anne achieved, there was no time for Cromwell, now acknowledged as his chief minister, to rest. The 1534 Parliament bristled with bills stopping payments to Rome, ensuring the cathedrals were brought under the King's jurisdiction, and, ominously, empowering the Crown to 'visit' (monitor) the monasteries. It was stated that this throwing off of Papal Supremacy was not to be taken to mean that England was departing from the 'articles of the

Catholic faith of Christendom' and, at this stage, no changes in religious practice were suggested.

The next important piece of legislation that Cromwell shepherded through Parliament in 1534 was the Act of Succession which, after a preamble denying papal supremacy, settled the succession on the children of Henry and his new queen, Anne's, heirs male, and thereafter on the heirs of any subsequent wife. Any subject over the age of fourteen could be called upon to swear an oath to uphold the Act.

It was decided that John Fisher, Bishop of Rochester, who had vigorously defended the marriage of Henry and Katharine, and Sir Thomas More, former Lord Chancellor, who was believed to be opposed to the Royal Supremacy, would be asked to swear the oath. Both men refused. Fisher boldly stated his grounds, and confirmed that he would sign an oath upholding the succession in accordance with the will of Parliament and the King, but would not deny Papal Supremacy. More also confirmed that he would swear to the proposed succession, but he would not sign the oath as it stood, although he gave no statement as to what he found objectionable. Both men were attainted in November 1534 and were sent to the Tower to think on their answers. Naturally, their property was confiscated.

At the end of the 1534 session of Parliament, three final Acts were drafted by Cromwell and Audley. The Act of Supremacy, which spelt out Royal Supremacy, rather than it just being part of the Act of Succession, the Treasons Act, which enlarged the concept of treason from acts to words, and a revised Act relating to annates, that began an audit of monastery land, through a Royal Commission. This session also introduced the acts which effectively amalgamated Wales into England, and created a unified state.

Early 1535 was taken up with matter of Bishop Fisher and Sir Thomas More. They were both still in the Tower, refusing to swear the oath of succession. More and Fisher were highly respected at home and abroad as pious, learned and virtuous. Our modern unease with More's treatment of 'heretics' did not raise any such doubts at the time. Repeatedly, Cromwell put pressure on them both.

On 7th May, 1535, he led a delegation to the Tower to request More to give his opinion on the Act of Supremacy, as the King had asked for it. More refused to discuss the matter, saying he had told the King and Cromwell what he thought when the matter was first mooted, and would say no more on the topic. Cromwell appears to have used his best endeavours to persuade More to accept the oath, saying the King would be merciful, and pointing out that, just because he was in prison, he need not think he could escape from obedience to the King. Cromwell then complained that More was encouraging others to disobey by his obstinacy. More only replied that

> 'I do nobody harm, I say none harm, I think none harm but wish everybody good. And if this be not enough to keep a man alive, in good faith, I long not to live. And I am dying already...And therefore my poor body is at the King's pleasure: would God my death might do him good.'

Cromwell spoke 'full gently' on hearing this, and assured More that no advantage would be taken of anything he had said.

However, Henry was not to be satisfied. On 3rd June, Cromwell returned, in a very much sterner mood. Pope Paul III, in a misguided attempt to improve the lot of Bishop Fisher, had created him a Cardinal. Henry was beside himself with rage, seeing the honouring of a disobedient subject as a deliberate provocation. He was determined that Fisher and More would conform.

The delegation, led by Cromwell, consisted this time of Lord Chancellor Audley, the Duke of Suffolk (Henry's brother-in-law) and the Earl of Wiltshire, Queen Anne's father. The men had a copy of the oath with them, and attempted to coerce More into either signing, or saying something treasonable that would call down the new Treason Act upon him. More was obdurate, and Cromwell was frustrated, telling More he liked him '*much worse*' than before. The Councillors then departed, and sent Sir Richard Rich, the Solicitor General, to remove More's books.

Cromwell drew up an indictment upon which More was tried at Westminster Hall. The first three counts of the indictment that effectively assumed guilt from refusal to give a reason for not signing the oath were dismissed by the court. The final charge was then the only matter left.

This charge, sworn to by Richard Rich, was that in a discussion about hypothetical cases, More had denied the Royal Supremacy. There were no other witnesses than the two men. More pointed out that, if he had not answered the King or his Councillors, he certainly wouldn't have shared his inmost thoughts with Rich, whom he heartily despised and accused of perjury.

The court returned a guilty verdict and More was beheaded on 6th July 1535, just after Bishop Fisher. So far as Cromwell was concerned, it was a job well done, even if he might have preferred Fisher and More to swear the oath to reduce opposition to the King.

Chapter 8: Cromwell & Anne Boleyn (1534 – 1536)

It is often stated that Cromwell was a client of the Boleyn family, and owed his rise to Anne's favour. However, this is quite clearly not the case – he came to the King's attention through his duties in relation to legal and conveyancing matters. The fact that he may have shared the Boleyns' inclination towards Church reform, might have made him more personally disposed to helping Henry with the annulment legislation, but that cannot be shown as the cause of his rise. His relationship with the new Queen was therefore one that developed over his time as the King's Councillor.

Anne was not popular, either with the public, or with the majority of the Court. Had she borne a son, all might have been forgiven, but the child who had been so eagerly awaited was a girl. Anne then had a miscarriage at some point during 1534, and her relationship with Henry continued to wax and wane. Chapuys reported as early as Christmas 1534 that Henry had consulted Cromwell as to whether he might throw off Anne, without having to return to Katharine, but since Henry and Anne had a notoriously volatile relationship, not much weight can be given to rumours at this point.

Chapuys also told Cromwell that the King and he would be held personally responsible by the Emperor should anything untoward happen to Katharine or Princess Mary, whom it was rumoured that Cromwell and /or Anne intended to have quietly dispatched.

During the late summer of 1535, Cromwell organised a summer progress for Henry, which took the court (minus Queen Anne, who was again pregnant and stayed at home to safeguard her health) to Wiltshire. Whilst there, the progress visited Wolf Hall, home of the Seymour family. The eldest Seymour daughter had, at some point, been a maid-of-honour to Katharine of Aragon, but was unnoticed by Henry at that time. Now, however, he fell in love with her. Since Anne was pregnant, he cannot have been anticipating matrimony at that point and Jane rejected his advances either from modesty, or policy. She was, nevertheless, given a place in Queen Anne's household, and Cromwell gave up his rooms at

Greenwich Palace to Jane's brother, Edward Seymour, to enable Henry to meet Jane in the bosom of her family.

January 1536 brought drama at court. Katharine of Aragon died, Henry was thrown violently from his horse, causing a concussion lasting some hours, and Anne miscarried *'of her saviour'*. Katharine now dead, there was the possibility of rapprochement with her nephew, the Emperor Charles, and a return to the traditional alliance between England and Burgundy. Had Anne borne a son, she would have been unlikely to accommodate such an alliance, but, with only a daughter, and Jane waiting in the wings, Anne was looking increasing expendable. It appears she had also quarrelled with Cromwell, threatening to have his head off his shoulders.

Cromwell began to investigate Anne and to sniff out gossip, which gave him enough material for the King to grant him a commission on 24 April, 1536 to enquire as to whether there was sufficient evidence to bring Anne to trial. The vast majority of observers, then and now, believe Anne to have been quite innocent of the charges of adultery and incest with five men that were brought against her. One confession (by Mark Smeaton) was obtained, probably through torture at Cromwell's own house. Historian George Bernard believes there may be some truth in the charges. True or not, matters were not to be left to chance – the court, headed by Anne's uncle, Norfolk, knew the sentence required, and an executioner had even been employed before Anne's trial began.

Cromwell, having tidily swept away another of Henry's problems, could bask in his title of Baron Cromwell and his new position of Lord Privy Seal, the office of which Anne's father had been deprived. Keen to hitch himself to the rising Seymour star, he arranged the marriage of his son, Gregory, to Elizabeth Seymour, Queen Jane's sister. His son was now brother-in-law to the King! Quite a step up for the son of a Putney blacksmith.

Chapter 9: Cromwell & Lady Mary

On the fall of Anne Boleyn, Henry's elder daughter, who had been degraded from the rank of Princess when Anne's daughter was born, wrote to Cromwell, requesting him to intercede for her with her father. She had consistently refused to accept the annulment of her parents' marriage, and had been disgraced and banished from her father's sight, to live, bullied and humiliated by Anne's relatives, in the household of the baby Elizabeth. Now, with Anne dead, she hoped to regain her father's favour. The fact that Lady Mary wrote to Cromwell in the summer of 1536 shows that even Henry's own daughter knew that, by now, Cromwell was the man he relied on to deal with day-to-day matters.

Cromwell must have been in a quandary. Whilst a King who had had his own wife executed might not baulk at meting out the same treatment to a disobedient daughter, even though he had once dearly loved her, such a step would be controversial, to say the least. In the summer of 1536, Henry had one adult daughter (Mary), an illegitimate son who was on his deathbed (Richmond) and a three-year-old daughter (Elizabeth), child of a woman executed for adultery. By custom, the succession, if none of these children were legitimate heirs, would fall to James V, King of Scots. If Mary were dead, that would be the most likely outcome, and deeply undesirable to all of England. In addition, proceeding against Mary might bring more than angry words from her cousin, Emperor Charles.

The best route out was to persuade Mary to accept the Act of Supremacy. Cromwell arranged for the Duke of Norfolk – a man of supreme tactlessness – the Earl of Sussex and a Bishop to visit Lady Mary and demand that she take the Oath of Supremacy. She refused.

Pressure had to be stepped up. Cromwell enlisted Chapuys, the Emperor's Ambassador, to point out to Mary the danger she stood in. Simultaneously, he wrote to her himself, saying:

'If you do not leave all sinister counsels, I take leave of you for ever and desire you to write to me no more, for I will never think you other than the most ungrateful, unnatural, and obstinate person living, both to God and your most dear and benign father.'

He accompanied this tirade with an obsequious letter for Mary to copy, acknowledging her father as Supreme Head of the Church, rejecting the Pope and agreeing that her parents' marriage had been unlawful and incestuous. Mary, finally bullied into submission, signed, whilst sending a message to Rome that it had been done with mental reservations.

On 5th July that year, Cromwell wrote to Bishop Gardiner of Winchester (later Mary's own Lord Chancellor) that 'my Lady Mary is a most obedient child to the King's Highness and is as conformable as any living faithful subject can be.'

Henry probably felt no small measure of gratitude to Cromwell for fixing this problem. Queen Jane, too, was grateful, and she immediately invited Mary to court and showered affection and gifts on her.

Chapter 10: Dissolution of the Monasteries

In 1534, Chapuys had noted that the King *'is very covetous of the goods of the Church, which he already considers his patrimony'* and, as was noted above, legislation in 1534 had implemented a valuation of all monastery lands. By October of that year, Cromwell was drafting a plan for how the wealth of the Church could be better disposed of, including the suppression of monastic houses with fewer than ten inmates, and diversion of the revenues to the Crown. The valuation survey was completed and compiled as '*Valor Ecclesiasticus*', the most wide-ranging survey of land since the Domesday Book. *Valor Ecclesiasticus* determined that the Church was worth some £800,000 per annum. As well as the valuations, the commissions to the surveyors had required them to report on the conduct of the monastic establishments.

Debate has continued for nearly five hundred years as to whether the monasteries were full of corruption, licentiousness and poverty of true religious life, or whether the odd bad example (inevitable in any organisation) was blown out of all proportion to condemn the monasteries, root and branch. Cromwell, personally, seems to have been antithetical to the concept of religious life and was thus mentally prepared to believe everything that confirmed his idea that the monasteries were anachronistic, decadent and potentially harbouring enemies of the King's supremacy, as well of course, as being awash with cash.

On 21st January 1535, the King gave Cromwell the office of Vicar-General, granting him the power to undertaken visitations (as inspections by ecclesiastical superiors were known) of all monasteries and colleges of priests. Cromwell appointed four men to carry out the tasks on his behalf. All of these men had worked with him previously and none of them were known for their scruples. A list of seventy-four questions was drawn up, to probe the innermost details of monastic life.

The initial plan was merely to close the smaller monasteries, and send those inmates who wished to continue in the religious life, to larger houses. It just so happened that plenty of evidence was found of corruption and bad practice in smaller houses, and when the bill to suppress them was introduced to Parliament, the Commons were so shocked, that cries of *'down with them'* were heard. Of the 300 or so monasteries below the threshold of £200 that had been set, 244 were dissolved, and 47 granted licences by the King to remain open. Crown revenues were handsomely increased.

With a huge bounty of land now free for redistribution, Cromwell was inundated with requests to persuade the King to grant some humble petition. The Court of Augmentations was instituted, which Richard Rich, Solicitor General, and Thomas Pope presided over as Chancellor and Treasurer. Cromwell and his men profited handsomely, but it is fair to say that many others of Henry's courtiers did too, and often those opposed in principle to the Royal Supremacy.

In 1536, Convocation, presided over by Cromwell as the King's Vicegerent in Spirituals, promulgated the Act of Ten Articles, a declaration of faith that challenged traditional Catholic teachings and began to give an opening to reformist, even Lutheran views. Cromwell then, on his own account, without consulting Convocation, gave orders for parish priests to preach on the Royal Supremacy, and to teach children the Creed and Paternoster in English as well as laying down rules for clerical behaviour, and stipulating how much priests should give in alms. An English Bible, too, was to be in every church from 1st August 1536.

Whatever the views of the Cromwell, the King, and his immediate circle on the legislative and religious developments of the period 1529-1536, many outside the south-east of England were very much less content. Rebellion broke out, first in Lincolnshire, and then, more seriously in Yorkshire. Suffice to say that, after a near-brush with civil war, during which Cromwell was repeatedly cast as the villain by the commons who complained, in time-honoured way, about the King's *'evil counsellors'* to avoid seeming to criticise the King, the rebels were overcome. The opinion, not just of the rebels, but of many of Henry's people was encapsulated in the words of Lord Darcy, before his execution.

'Cromwell, it is thou that art the very original and chief causer of all this rebellion and mischief and art likewise causer of the apprehension of us that be noble men and dost daily earnestly travail to bring us to one end and to strike of our heads and I trust that, or [before] thou die, though thou wouldst procure all the noblemen's heads within the realm to be striken off, that still there one head remain that shall strike of thy head.'

Nevertheless, Cromwell was riding high. The disturbances of the Pilgrimage of Grace meant that coerced dissolutions of the larger monasteries was politically impossible, but enough pressure was brought to bear for them to surrender voluntarily. Cromwell also continued to act as the King's right hand man, particularly in the passage of the Act of Proclamations which, despite opposition from the Lords, who feared its use might be arbitrary, confirmed that the King's Proclamations, in relation to statutes passed by Parliament, had the same force as the statutes.

In 1539, too, many of Cromwell's enemies were disposed of in connection with the Exeter Conspiracy. It seemed that the Lord Privy Seal could not fail.

The tide, however, was about to turn.

Chapter 11: Cromwell's Downfall (1539 – 1540)

Henry VIII was widowed in October 1537, when Queen Jane died in childbed. Cromwell almost immediately sought a suitable replacement – preferably a wealthy, healthy princess who would counterbalance the threats to England from the France and the Empire, which were still making noises about invading England to restore Papal authority. He lit upon the sisters of Wilhelm, Duke of Cleves, as likely candidates. Cleves, like England had thrown off Papal authority, but had not gone far down the road of Lutheranism. It was also one of the duchies that made up the Empire, so an alliance would be bound to irritate Emperor Charles.

Hans Holbein, Henry's court painter, and probably a friend of Cromwell, was sent to paint the Ladies Amelia and Anna. The portrait that was delivered of Lady Anna was so delightful that Henry was prepared to ally with a more religiously radical regime. The wedding was arranged and Anna of Cleves duly arrived in England. Henry, not quite as young and handsome as he had once been, raced to meet her, disguised as a merchant. Anna, sick and weary after a dismal channel crossing, not recognising in the corpulent, aging, burgess the romantic prince of her dreams, greeted him coldly and failed to exert any charm she may have had. Henry was not impressed. Always gentlemanly in his demeanour to ladies, he treated Anna with the utmost courtesy, but he expressed his private feelings to Cromwell saying that '*She is nothing so fair as she hath been reported*' and that he would not put his head into the '*yoke*' of marriage with her, if there were any alternative.

No alternative could be found and the marriage went ahead. No doubt Cromwell was hoping that Henry would overcome his personal repugnance and settle down with Anna. But Henry could not overcome his feelings – and was soon engaged in a more pleasing relationship. The Duke of Norfolk's niece, Katheryn Howard, was one of Anna's new maids-of-honour and the King became infatuated.

Norfolk, who had resented Cromwell becoming Henry's chief minister instead of himself, and Cromwell's old sparring partner, Bishop Gardiner, who was implacably imposed to the innovation in religion, with which Cromwell was increasingly associated, saw their chance. Cromwell's patronage of Robert Barnes, an ardent reformer who was accused of heresy, was an opportunity for Gardiner to tar Cromwell with the same brush, knowing that Henry, who was becoming increasingly concerned about a drift away from Catholic doctrine, would not tolerate heresy in his chief minister.

Through a masterly handling of the opening session of the new Parliament in April 1540, Cromwell managed to diffuse the growing religious controversy. He also resigned his position of Secretary to two of his supporters, to try to increase his support on the Privy Council. Norfolk and Gardiner, however, were just biding their time.

Cromwell was promoted again, to be Earl of Essex and Lord Great Chamberlain, a largely ceremonial post and the French Ambassador believed him to be as high in Henry's favour as ever. But on 10th June 1540, the blow fell. Cromwell attended a Privy Council meeting at Westminster. The King was absent and the other Councillors had all assembled before Cromwell's arrival. On entrance, he looked for a seat, and was told that there was no seat for him amongst gentlemen. Norfolk then arrested him for high treason and personally tore off the collar of St George that Cromwell wore as a Knight of the Garter. Not surprisingly, Cromwell protested his innocence, but no notice was taken and he was dragged off to the Tower. Norfolk would not have taken such a step without Henry's approval, and yet it is difficult to believe that Henry can really have given credence to such spurious claims as that Cromwell wanted to marry Henry's daughter, Mary, and seize the throne. He must have been convinced that Cromwell's repeated conferences with the German Lutherans meant that Cromwell himself was infected with '*heresy*'. If that were the case, there could be no mercy.

Cranmer wrote to Henry, almost protesting Cromwell's innocence:

'Who cannot be sorrowful and amazed that he should be a traitor against Your Majesty – he whose surety was only by Your Majesty...who studied always to put set forward whatsoever was Your Majesty's pleasure...For who shall Your Grace trust hereafter, if you might not trust him?

Cromwell wrote to Henry from the Tower, *'with the quaking hand of the most sorrowful heart of your most sorrowful subject and most humble servant and prisoner.'*

He had never knowingly committed any offence against the King, and if, in the course of his multifarious tasks he had accidentally broken any law, he begged for mercy.

Henry believed that Cromwell might still be of some use to him. He wanted his marriage to Anna annulled and Cromwell could help him to achieve that end. Not only was the delicious morsel of Katheryn Howard being laid before him daily by Norfolk and Gardiner, but the political motive for the marriage had also disappeared, as François I of France and the Emperor Charles were once again fighting for Milan.

Cromwell confirmed that Henry had entered the marriage unwillingly, and not consummated it. The marriage was annulled, and Anna, after initial hesitancy, accepted the King's terms with a good grace, remaining in England, honoured and respected, as the King's *'sister'* and friend. Cromwell, although just as keen to please, received no benefit from his help. An Act of Attainder had already been passed, condemning him to death. Nevertheless, he wrote again to Henry pleading for *'mercy, mercy, mercy'*.

His words fell on deaf ears. Unlike Wolsey, with whom Henry had had a warm, personal relationship, Cromwell was no more to him than a servant. There was no hesitation. Cromwell, now stripped of his new titles, was executed on 28th July 1540. In the speech from the scaffold purported to be his, he confirmed his faith in the Catholic Church, and all of its sacraments. After a bungled execution, requiring at least three blows, his head was displayed on London Bridge, no doubt as a mark of gratitude for a man who had served his king so faithfully. The King mourned by marrying Katheryn Howard the same day.

Aspects of Thomas Cromwell's Life

Chapter 12: Cromwell & the English Bible

Contrary to popular belief, there was no absolute prohibition on Bibles in the vernacular prior to the Reformation. There had been a translation into French as early as the late thirteenth century and into Czech in the fourteenth century. The reality was that, before the printing press, and the growth of lay education in the fifteenth century, almost the only readers were the clergy, and the more academically inclined nobles, who could all read Latin, so there was little market for Bibles in any other language.

The first printed Bible was an edition of the Vulgate (ie the standard Latin Bible, first translated in the late fourth century by St Jerome and his assistants, from the original Hebrew, Aramaic and Greek). It was printed 1454, in Mainz and was designed to be look just like a hand-written manuscript. This was followed by a printed version of a Czech translation in 1488.

Towards the end of the fifteenth century, scholars, particularly Erasmus of Rotterdam, questioned the validity of Jerome's translation, and Erasmus went back to the original Greek to produce a revised edition of the Gospels – a work that produced some controversy, as potentially challenging Catholic orthodoxy. Simultaneously, in the spirit of renewal of religion that Erasmus and the other Humanists were fostering, there was pressure for translations of the Bible into local languages to enable Christians to read the word of God for themselves. The Church authorities were somewhat suspicious, but translations were not forbidden per se, they just had to be licensed by the appropriate authority – usually the Primate or a resident Papal Legate.

In England, there were early Anglo-Saxon translations of part of the Gospels, but the first full translation had been done in the late fourteenth century, by John Wycliffe. Wycliffe had been condemned as a heretic, and his translation was forbidden from 1407 onward. His followers, known as '*Lollards*', continued as an underground movement, and preserved copies of his Bible, despite the fact that being caught in possession of it attracted a death sentence.

The concern over the Lollard heresy had led to a repressive attitude in England to all translations of the Bible. In Europe, translations were appearing in the 1520s in countries that would remain within the Catholic fold, as well as those moving towards Lutheranism. The New Testament was published in French in 1523, and the whole Bible in 1530 by Lefevre, under the protection of François I and his sister, Marguerite, later Queen of Navarre; simultaneously, Luther's translation of 1523 was an early best-seller in Germany. During the 1520s and 1530s translations appeared in Swiss, Dutch and Tuscan.

There was a growing demand for an English translation to enable the Word of God to be read by all. Supporters of the Bible in English during the 1520s were called '*evangelicals*', they were not necessarily Lutherans, and many who supported a more Biblically based faith never left the Catholic Church. However, there was one man whose desire for an English translation was only part of his wider conversion to the more personal faith espoused by the Reformers – William Tyndale.

Tyndale, a notable scholar and linguist, hoped to make a full English translation from the original Greek and Hebrew. He approached Cuthbert Tunstall, Bishop of London, in 1523 for a licence. Tunstall, although he was himself a scholar and a collaborator with Erasmus, felt that Tyndale was too radical and refused to be involved with his plans.

Tyndale left for the Low Countries, and began translating part of the New Testament in 1524. A second, full, translation followed in 1526, printed in Worms. Copies of Tyndale's work were smuggled into England, in bales of cloth, at 9d per set of octavo sheets. There had been no softening on the position that possession of unlicensed English Bibles was punishable by death. However, the growth of the printing press meant that the sheer quantity of volumes that could be brought in rendered its dissemination unstoppable.

Bishop Tunstall, in an ill-considered act, burnt Tyndale's works after condemning them as heretical at St Paul's Cathedral. The sight of Bibles being burnt made many uneasy, even those who were not inclined towards Tyndale's Lutheran views, which supported Justification by Faith alone and undermined the Catholic belief in prayers for the dead.

Cromwell is usually described as a radical in religious matters, an early Protestant (although the term was not in common currency until after his death), but there were many shades of evangelicalism between the strict conservatism of men such as Bishop Gardiner, Cromwell's nemesis, and *'heretics'* such as Tyndale. Whereas Anne Boleyn and her family, and Archbishop Cranmer are referred to by Eustache Chapuys, that inveterate reporter of gossip, as '*Lutherans*' he does not use that term of Cranmer.

Cromwell's Will, made after September 1532, asks for the intercession of the Virgin and the Saints, allocates money for several houses of friars, and for prayers for his soul, a traditional Catholic practice that by 1532 was excoriated by Tyndale and Luther. His stance was certainly anti-clerical - the Chronicler, Edward Hall, himself having reformist tendencies recorded that Cromwell '*could not abide the snoffyng pride of some prelates*', but whether he supported doctrinal changes in the early 1530s is questionable.

Cromwell moved in intellectual circles, and a later correspondent wrote that he treasured the memory of '*divers dinners*' at Cromwell's home at Austin Friars where he had heard '*such communication which were the verye cause of the begynninge of my conversion*' but he also maintained friendships with conservatives such as Edmund Bonner, later Bishop of London under Mary.

Exactly why and when Cromwell himself first read an English Bible is unknown. According to John Foxe, on one of Cromwell's trips to Rome in the 1510s he had memorised Erasmus' New Testament. This would certainly suggest a lively interest in religion, beyond just form, and together with his naturally inquiring mind would probably have led him to read Tyndale's work. With his contacts in the cloth trade he would have had easy access to a contraband copy, most likely through his friend and associate in Antwerp, Stephen Vaughan, whom Cromwell later warned that he was becoming suspect for Lutheran views.

Whether or not Cromwell entertained Lutheran doctrinal views cannot be proven but what can be, is his commitment to the Bible in English. Foxe, in his '*Book of Martyrs*' wrote that Cromwell's

> '*whole life was nothing els, but a continuall care and travaile how to advaunce and futher the right knowledge of the Gospell*'.

In 1534, the Convocation of Clergy, now the governing body of the English Church, under the King, petitioned the monarch for a full translation of the Bible for the edification of his subjects. It was suggested that Tyndale might be employed to do it, on condition that he ceased to write the offensive polemics against the King's annulment that had poured from his pen. Henry, although he was prepared to consider an English Bible, was apoplectic at the thought of encouraging Tyndale whom, according to Cromwell, he considered to be '*replete with venomous envy, rancour and malice*'.

A translator more acceptable to the King would have to be found.

Miles Coverdale was a Cambridge graduate, who was ordained priest in 1514, before becoming an Augustinian Friar. Amongst his circle of acquaintances were Robert Barnes, later burnt for heresy, Sir Thomas More, and Cromwell. Coverdale's views became more evangelical as time passed, and he spent the years 1528 – 1534 abroad. By 1535 he had completed a translation of the Bible, which was the first full translation, and much of which found its way into the King James' Authorised Version of 1611. Two more editions of the 1537 work were published, and, although it was not an official translation, it appeared in many parish churches from 1st August 1537, from which date all churches were to have an English Bible.

The title page, designed by Holbein, shows Henry VIII brandishing the Sword of Justice in one hand, and giving the Word of God to his bishops with the other. The work is dedicated to Henry saying

'He only under God is the Chief Head of all the congregation of the Church'.

Coverdale was now free to return to England, where he arranged a further printing of his New Testament, bound together with a copy of the Vulgate.

Another translation appeared in 1537, also licensed for use. This was the Matthew Bible, a combination of translations from Coverdale, Tyndale and Thomas Matthews, chaplain to the Merchant Adventurers in Antwerp. This Bible was Archbishop Cranmer's personal favourite and was to be used until the Bishops should 'set forth a better translation' although he admitted to Cromwell that this would probably not be achieved until 'the day after Domesday.'

In fact, Cranmer had already taken steps for a new translation and allocated sections to different bishops for translation. The fact that one of these was the conservative Gardiner, Bishop of Winchester, confirms that a desire for an English Bible was not a hallmark of Lutheranism, especially as Gardiner, unlike many of the others, completed his section – the Gospels of Luke and John.

Nevertheless, it was agreed, presumably between the King, Cranmer and Cromwell, that the first authorised translation would be a revision of the Matthew Bible, supervised by Coverdale and with additions from Sebastian Munster's rendition of the Old Testament from the original Hebrew.

On 5th September 1538 Cromwell, as the King's Vicegerent in Spirituals, ordered that the Bible be available in all churches by All Saints' Day (1st November), although, in the event, the new translation was delayed.

There was a lack of facilities for printing such a large work, and the copies needed, in London, so Bishop Gardiner was asked to obtain a licence from François I for its production in France. The licence was granted, but the French Inquisitor-General smelt heresy and tried to have the book impounded. Fortunately, Coverdale and the printer, Richard Grafton, managed to escape France with the type, the printing press and the sheets completed to date. The work was finished and issued in London in April 1539.

The resulting tome was known as 'The Great Bible' not for its brilliance, but for its size – it was to be of a size to be read and consulted by every parishioner.

Cromwell's desire to see the Bible in English, available to everyone, cannot be denied, yet he saw no harm in turning a profit from it too. He invested £800 in the printing, and obtained a monopoly of the profits of the first five years of print runs. The book was to be of the largest volume, printed on good quality paper, and to cost 10 shillings – Cranmer had thought 13s 4d reasonable. The parish priest and his flock were to share the purchase price between them. Whilst unlearned folk were not to dispute on the content of the Bible, everyone was to be encouraged to read *'the very lively word of God that every Christian person is bound to embrace, believe and follow'*.

Chapter 13: Following the Footsteps of Thomas Cromwell

The numbers in the article below correspond to those on the map which follows.

Thomas Cromwell came from a modest background, so tracking his movements during the early part of his life is not easy. The Cromwells were originally from Norwell in Nottinghamshire (1) but by the time of his father's birth, they were settled in south-west London. Thomas was brought up in Putney, where they had a house not far from the River Thames in Brewhouse Lane (2). An exact date for Cromwell leaving home is not known, but it is likely to have been around the turn of the sixteenth century. For the next ten years or so, he travelled in Europe, first in the French army, although he apparently left after the overwhelming defeat at Garigliano in 1503, and then in Florence, the centre of the cultural renaissance that was spreading across Europe. Following that, he lived and worked in Antwerp for a period, during which time he made a range of contacts with merchants involved in the cloth industry.

On returning to London, around 1512, he seems to have set up home in Fenchurch Street (3). The street is still there, but no trace remains of any sixteenth centuries homes. It is likely he lived here with his wife, Elizabeth Wykys, whom he married some time before 1516, as he developed a career as lawyer, cloth merchant and moneylender.

One of Cromwell's earliest recorded legal clients was the Guild of the Church of Our Lady, Boston, Lincolnshire (4) – the church itself is now known as the Boston Stump. He made a successful visit to Rome on the Guild's behalf.

When Cromwell entered Wolsey's service, sometime around 1519, he was employed on property and financial matters. His most important role, which he carried out with remarkable diligence, was the dissolution of the religious houses whose revenues were to be diverted to the building of Wolsey's colleges at Ipswich (5) and Oxford (6). He also oversaw the building works, and the entire setting up of the new foundations. This activity necessitated a good deal of riding about between the various locations involved.

In 1523, Cromwell entered Parliament. At that time Parliament usually met in Westminster Hall (7), the fabulous hall dating from the reign of Richard II, that still remains, and has witnessed so much of English and British history. The Parliament lasted seventeen weeks, and Cromwell wrote to a friend that matters ended pretty much as they had begun.

Whilst in Wolsey's household, Cromwell would have spent a good deal of time at York Place (8). This was rebuilt by Henry VIII as the royal palace of Whitehall. Cromwell was closely involved in both the legal niceties required for Henry to have a valid title to the lands, and also the refurbishment works.

Hampton Court (9) too was a place where Cromwell would have spent a good deal of time, both in service to Wolsey, and later, when it was one of Henry VIII's favourite palaces.

Cromwell was aware of how unpopular Wolsey had made himself through his extravagance and magnificent style of life, thought by the nobility to be quite incompatible with his humble beginnings. Cromwell was certainly not going to make that mistake. He had a house near the convent of the Austin Friars (10) in the City of London. Again, the street name remains, but there are no traces of sixteenth century life. Here he seems to have spent much of his personal life, wining and dining the city merchants who were his friends. He also had an official residence at Rolls House, Chancery Lane (11), in his capacity as Master of the Rolls. This has since been replaced with the Maughan Library, a neo-gothic fantasy.

Service to the King had its rewards – Cromwell built up an impressive property portfolio in and around London. Amongst his properties, he had a house at Stepney (12), where he interrogated Mark Smeaton in a quest to find evidence against Anne Boleyn, and estates out of town at Mortlake (13) and Ewhurst (14). No traces of these survive.

Although he had property outside the capital London, Cromwell was always a Londoner, and even in death, he remained within a stone's throw of the City. His final days were spent in the Tower of London (15), and his remains lie there still.

Key to Map

1. Norwell, Nottinghamshire

2. Brewhouse Lane, Putney, London

3. Fenchurch, London

4. St Botolph's Church, Boston, Lincolnshire

5. Ipswich

6. Christ Church, Oxford

7. Westminster Hall, London

8. York Place, London

9. Hampton Court Palace, Surrey

10. Austin Friars, London

11. Rolls House, London

12. Mortlake, Greater London

13. Stepney, London

14. Ewhurst, Surrey

15. Tower of London, London

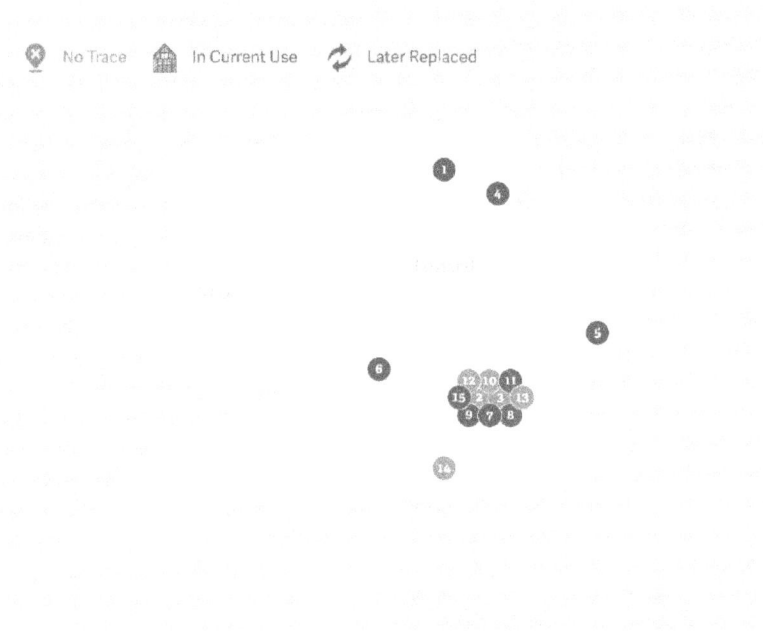

Chapter 14: Book Review

Cromwell was frequently referred to in contemporary correspondence and also makes an appearance in Cavendish's *'Life of Wolsey'* and Foxe's *'Acts and Monuments'*. A comprehensive study of his life and letters was undertaken by Merriman in 1901. He came to the fore again in G R Elton's reappraisal of the Tudor period in the 1950s. Current biographies are by Hutchinson (2006), Borman (2014) and Everett (2015). We have reviewed Everett's biography here.

The Rise of Thomas Cromwell

Author: Michael Everett

Publisher: Yale University Press

In a nutshell A truly comprehensive study of Cromwell's early career, both before and after he joined the King's Privy Council. Ideal for anyone who wants to see a biography built up from the details of daily activities.

When I saw that a new biography had been published of Cromwell, I couldn't help a groan – I had already immersed myself in several other works for our Person of the Month feature, and I did not want to read the same facts again, in a different format. However, I could not have been more wrong, this book is well worth reading – no matter what you have read on Cromwell, you will find something new here.

Everett has taken a completely new approach, and concentrates on Cromwell's practical life as a solicitor, conveyancer, surveyor and receiver of rents, first for Wolsey, then for Henry VIII. The basis of Everett's thesis, is that Cromwell didn't make an instant leap from nobody to Henry's right hand man. His position was built up by proving his capabilities in financial and administrative matters related to Crown revenues and building works, before he began to be involved in political affairs. He did not, as is sometimes claimed, start out with the ambition of replacing Wolsey as the King's chief minister, rather, his efficiency and dispatch in business made his rise inevitable in a court where the King and the other senior councillors tended to delegate.

Everett is an absolute stickler for proof, nothing that is not documented is asserted, although different perspectives are discussed.

The book makes two points that are well worth considering – first, Everett draws our attention to the risk of assuming that Cromwell's role was greater than anyone else's, just because of the mass of documentation that has survived. Cromwell's papers were seized on his downfall and became part of the Crown archive, and because they are so voluminous, they are relied on extensively. Would a different picture emerge if a similar hoard of papers were discovered, relating to another minister or courtier?

The second point, which emerges from the details that Everett has so painstakingly drawn together, is that Cromwell acted in concert with others, particularly in the early days as a Privy Councillor and he also shows that Cromwell, although influential with the King, certainly did not get everything he wanted. Henry distributed patronage to reflect his own needs – he would listen to Cromwell, but he listened to others, too.

Everett's style is clear and matter-of-fact. He has obviously spent a huge amount of time and care on collating original sources and reviewing accepted datings of letters and documents. There are no flights of fancy, or attempts to understand people's inner motivations where there is no evidence – as he says, amongst all of the papers, there is almost nothing relating to Cromwell's personal life. The sheer quantity of detail means the book drags a little in the middle, but this is an academic study, not a work of popular history, so perhaps some tedium is inevitable.

Although the book is very factual, what I derived from it will influence how I read other biographies in future. Everett demonstrates, although he does not actually articulate the argument, that we have a tendency to read earlier events in the light of later happenings. Thus, because Cromwell became all-powerful earlier biographers infer that he set out with this ambition in mind. Everett avoids this trap by writing forward, rather than with hindsight, giving a much more realistic picture of how life unfolds for most of us – being in the right place at the right time is worth any number of plans.

Next time I read any biography, I will try to erase from my mind any knowledge of the future that will lead to misinterpretation of the present.

Disappointingly, Everett stops in 1534, before the exciting events of the downfall of Anne Boleyn, the Dissolution of the Monasteries, the Pilgrimage of Grace and the Exeter Conspiracy. I sincerely hope he brings out a second volume to cover Cromwell's involvement in these momentous events.

Bibliography

Calendar of State Papers Simancas, British History Online (HMSO, 1892) Hume, Martin A S, ed.,

Calendar of State Papers: Venice <http://www.british-history.ac.uk/cal-state-papers/venice/vol2/vii-lxi> [accessed 7 October 2015]

Letters and Papers, Foreign and Domestic, of the Reign of Henry VIII: Preserved in the Public Record Office, the British Museum, and Elsewhere in England (United Kingdom: British History Online, 2014) https://www.british-history.ac.uk/letters-papers-hen8/ Brewer, John Sherren, and James Gairdner,

Select Documents Of English Constitutional History, ed. by George Burton Adams and Morse H Stephens (United States: Kessinger Publishing, 2007)

Borman, Tracy, *Thomas Cromwell: The Untold Story of Henry VIII's Most Faithful Servant* (United Kingdom: Hodder & Stoughton, 2014)

Cavendish, George, *Life of Cardinal Wolsey* (Forgotten Books 2009)

Creighton, Mandell, *Cardinal Wolsey* (Bibliolife 28 Jan 2009)

De Lisle, Leanda, *Tudor: The Family Story* (United Kingdom: Chatto & Windus, 2013)

Dodds, M. H. and Dodds, R. (1971) *The Pilgrimage of Grace, 1536-1537 and the Exeter Conspiracy, 1538*. London: Frank Cass Publishers.

Ellis, Henry, *Original Letters, Illustrative of English History: Including Numerous Royal Letters: From Autographs in the British Museum, the State Paper Office, and One or Two Other Collections.*, 1st edn (New York: Printed for Harding, Triphook, & Lepard, 1824)

Everett, Michael, *The Rise of Thomas Cromwell: Power and Politics in the Reign of Henry VIII 1485 - 1534,* Kindle (New Haven and London: Yale University Press, 2015)

Fletcher, A. and Vernon, L. (1973) *Tudor Rebellions (Seminar Studies in History).* 2nd edn. Harlow: Longman.

Fraser, Antonia, *The Six Wives of Henry VIII*, First (London: Weidenfeld & Nicolson, 1992)

Foxe, John, *The Acts and Monuments of John Foxe: A New and Complete Edition: With a Preliminary Dissertation by the Rev. George Townsend* (London: R.R. Seeley and W. Burnside, 1837)

Gwyn, Peter, *The King's Cardinal: The Rise and Fall of Thomas Wolsey* (Pimlico 1992)

Hall, Edward, *Hall's Chronicle.* (S.l.: Ams Press, 1909)

Hayward, Maria, ed., *The Great Wardrobe Accounts of Henry VII and Henry VIII* (United Kingdom: London Record Society, 2012)

Holinshed, Raphael, *Holinshed's Chronicles of England, Scotland & Ireland* (United Kingdom: AMS Press, 1997)

Hutchinson, Robert, *Thomas Cromwell: The Rise and Fall of Henry VIII's Most Notorious Minister* (London: Weidenfeld & Nicolson, 2007)

Jerdan, William, ed., *Rutland Papers. Original Documents Illustrative of the Courts and Times of Henry VII. and Henry VIII. Selected from the Private Archives of His Grace the Duke of Rutland* (Leopold Classic Library, 2015)

Jones, D. (2014) *The Hollow Crown: The Wars of the Roses and the Rise of The Tudors.* 1st edn. United Kingdom: Faber & Faber Non-Fiction.

Merriman, Roger Bigelow, *Life and Letters of Thomas Cromwell: 2 Volumes* (Oxford Scholarly Classics) (Oxford: Oxford University Press, USA, 1901)

Ridley, Jasper, *Statesman and the Fanatic: Thomas Wolsey and Thomas More* London Constable 1982

Scarisbrick, J. J., *Henry VIII (Yale English Monarchs Series)* (Yale University Press 2 April 1997)

Starkey, David, *The Reign of Henry VIII: Personalities and Politics* (Vintage 3 October 2002)

Strickland, A. and Strickland, E. (2011) *Lives of the Queens of England from the Norman Conquest: Volume 3 & 4*. United Kingdom: Cambridge University Press (Virtual Publishing).

Strype, John, Annals of the Reformation and Establishment of Religion and Other Various Occurrences in the Church of England Etc. (Oxford: Clarendon Press, 1824),

Weir, Alison, *Henry VIII: King and Court* (London: Jonathan Cape, 2001)

Weir, Alison, *The Six Wives of Henry VIII*, 1st edn (London: Random House UK Distribution, 1991)

Williams, Neville, *Henry VIII and His Court*. (London: Littlehampton Book Services, 1971)

Williams, Neville, *The Cardinal and the Secretary: Thomas Wolsey and Thomas Cromwell* (United States: Macmillan, 1976)

www.ingramcontent.com/pod-product-compliance
Lightning Source LLC
Chambersburg PA
CBHW020522030426
42337CB00011B/519